INUYASHA

VOL. 55 Shonen Sunday Edition

STORY AND ART BY

RUMIKO TAKAHASHI

CONTENTS

THE STORY THUS FAR

Long ago, in the "Warring States" era of Japan's Muromachi period, dog-like half demon Inuyasha attempted to steal the Shikon Jewel—or "Jewel of Four Souls"—from a village. The village priestess, Kikyo, put a stop to his thievery with an enchanted arrow. Pinned to a tree, Inuyasha fell into a deep sleep, while mortally wounded Kikyo took the jewel with her into her funeral pyre. Years passed...

In the present day, Kagome, a Japanese high school girl, is pulled down into a well and transported into the past. There she discovers trapped Inuyasha—and frees him.

When the Shikon Jewel mysteriously reappears, demons attack. In the ensuing battle, the jewel *shatters*!

Now Inuyasha is bound to Kagome with a powerful spell, and the grudging companions must battle to reclaim the shattered shards of the Shikon Jewel to keep them out of evil hands...

LAST VOLUME When Kikyo's spirit saves Kohaku by abandoning the Shikon Jewel, Naraku begins to absorb the jewel and repels his attackers by dividing and manipulating them with illusions. Naraku unleashes Inuyasha's demon half, in hopes he will turn on Kagome. Inuyasha resists, but then Magatsuhi possesses Inuyasha's body! Sesshomaru battles Magatsuhi for his brother's body and soul, but it is Kagome's peril that brings Inuyasha back to himself...

INUYASHA
Half-demon hybrid, son of a human mother and demon father. His necklace is enchanted, allowing Kagome to control him with a word.

KAGOME
Modern-day Japanese schoolgirl who can travel back and forth between the past and present through an enchanted well.

SESSHOMARU
Inuyasha's pure-blood demon half brother. They have the same demon father.

MAGATSUHI
A monstrous demon who dwells inside the Shikon Jewel but can sometimes escape to wreak havoc on everyone.

NARAKU
Enigmatic demon mastermind behind the miseries of nearly everyone in the story. He has the power to create multiple incarnations of himself from his body.

BYAKUYA
A powerful sorcerer and master of illusions created by Naraku.

MIROKU
A Buddhist monk cursed with a mystical "Wind Tunnel" imbedded in his hand that both functions as a weapon and is slowly killing him.

SANGO
A demon slayer from the village where the Shikon Jewel originated.

RIN
An orphaned girl devoted to Sesshomaru. He once resurrected her with Tenseiga. She brings out the best in him.

SCROLL 1

ENTRAPPED

HSH
KAGOME...

...I SWORE...
...TO DEFEND YOU WITH MY LIFE!!

INU-YASHA...
...BROKE FREE OF MAGATSUHI'S SPELL WITHOUT USING HIS BLADE?!

WIMP

HOOO...

UHH...

SHH...

YOU... RECOG-NIZE ME?
INUYASHA...? YOU SAVED ME...?

...YOUR VOICE...
I... HEARD...

INU-YASHA... WHERE'S TETSU-SAIGA...?
I DON'T KNOW...IT KEPT FALLING...

WHAT NOW, MAGA-TSUHI?
SEEMS THE HALF DEMON IS HARDER TO CONTROL THAN YOU THOUGHT.
HOOOOO

SESSHO-MARU...

AND YOU, SESSHO-MARU...
DO YOU WISH ME TO ABANDON INUYASHA?

IF MAGATSUHI DEPARTS INUYASHA'S BODY...

HE MIGHT TRY TO POSSESS *ME* NEXT...

WHEN HE LEAVES INUYASHA...
I'LL HAVE ONLY A MOMENT TO ACT...

HSH...
!

RUN!

I... I CAN'T!

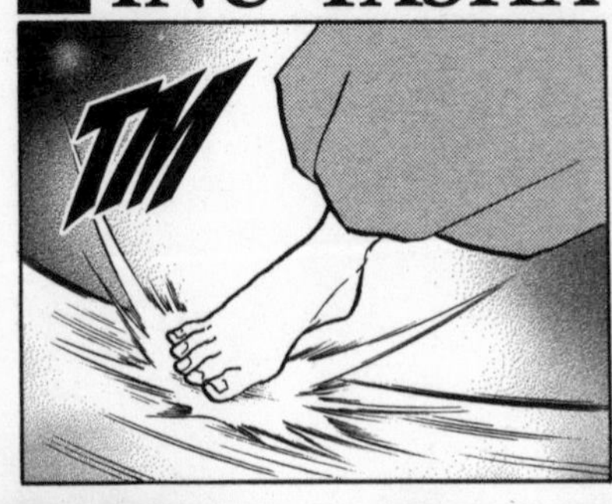
TM

HE'S GOING INTO KAGOME!

INU-YASHA...
VAH
VSH

HEH HEH HEH... TOO LATE!
HOOOOO
GO AS FAR AWAY FROM HER AS YOU WILL...

A PART OF ME IS ALREADY INSIDE HER!
OOO...

SESSHO-MARU...
IF YOU WISH TO CUT ME DOWN WITH TENSEIGA, YOU HAVE ONLY ONE CHOICE.

YOU MUST DESTROY ALL FLESH THAT I INHABIT...
...AND SO YOU MUST TEAR BOTH INUYASHA AND KAGOME APART.

DAMN HIM...
I'M... BLACKING OUT AGAIN...

HOOO
TING...

VSH

TETSU-SAIGA?!

HWUP
B-DMM

THE DRAGON SCALES...?!

HOOO...

HSSS...
BOMM

WHAT?!

I'M BEING PUSHED OUT OF BOTH OF THEM?!

SHOO

HOOOOO
DMM

WRL

I CAN'T...
...ENTER ANYONE... NOR RUN AWAY!
HOOO

I'VE GOT HIM TRAPPED...
...IN MY DEMON VORTEX!

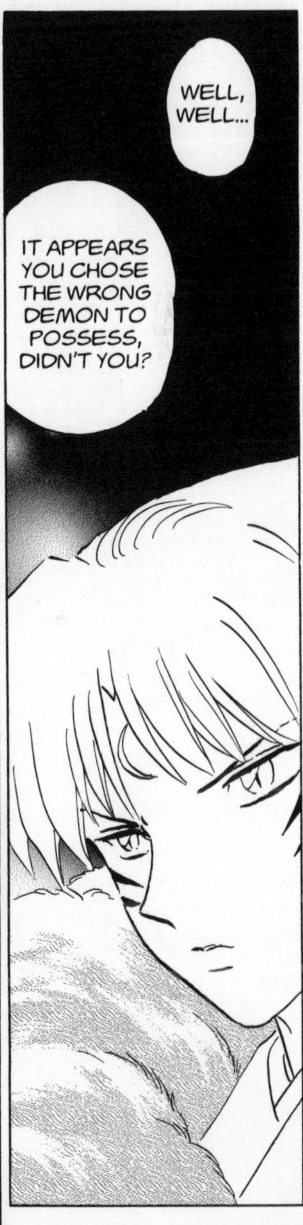

TENSEIGA!

VSH

SHAH
MAGATSUHI—
DIE!!

NO...
I WON'T BE VANQUISHED BY THE ENERGY OF...
SWOO...
...A HALF DEMON!
KLAK...
WOOO

BMMM

KAGO-
ME...

I FEEL
LIKE...
...A FOG IS
LIFTING...
B-DMM...

SCROLL 2

THE LIGHT REBORN

MAGATSUHI IS FINISHED.
SWOOO
THE SPIRIT POWERS HE SEALED AWAY... THEY'RE COMING...
B-DMM

B-DMMM
KAGO-ME...

WHOOM
!

OH!!

KAGO-ME!!
VM

B-DMM
FMP

SWOO...

WOOO...

I'M SO GLAD...
...YOU'RE *YOU* AGAIN.
I'M BACK TO MYSELF...
...THANKS TO YOUR POWERS.

B-DMM
IT'S BECAUSE SESSHOMARU CUT MAGATSUHI DOWN.
THANK YOU...

B-DMM
... SESSHO-MARU...

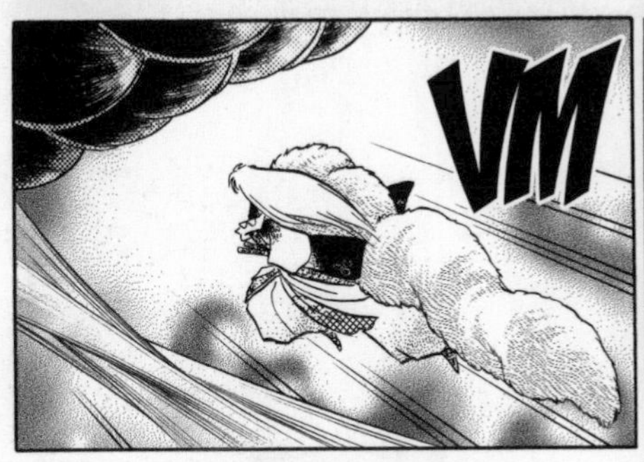
VM

RIN... I CAN SMELL HER AGAIN!
IT'S AS IF A FOG HAS BEEN LIFTED!

ARE KAGOME'S SPIRIT POWERS...
...DISPELLING NARAKU'S AURA?!

KRK KRK
BDMM
!

KRK KRK

FZZ
WAK

ZZZZ

SO, NARAKU...
IT SEEMS YOU
CAN'T HIDE YOUR
TRUE SELF
ANYMORE.

BDMM

W-WHAT'S HAPPENING?!
HAS NARAKU SPOTTED US?!

!
KRK KRK

YAGH!
WMP
LORD JAKEN!
KRK KRK

WMP
AAAAA!!
SHIP-PO!

IT'S OKAY, KOHAKU!
THIS IS NOTH—

SPLCH SPLCH

KOHAKU?! JAKEN?! WHERE ARE YOU?!
B-DMM
WAAAH!

B-DMM
LORD JAKEN!
SHIPPO!

WHAT'S ...
...HAPPEN-ING?!

YES.
THESE TREMORS...

LET'S GO, INUYASHA!
...TO THE SHIKON JEWEL!

B-DOMM

I THINK NARAKU'S DONE MESSING WITH US...
HE'S COMING AFTER US PERSONALLY NOW!
TMP

VSH

TING...

BOM-MM

IT IS THE LIGHT OF HOPE...

...TO INUYASHA AND HIS ALLIES.

THEN WHY DON'T I USE IT...

...TO LURE THESE MOTHS TO THEIR DOOM?

BDMM

BOOM
!

LIGHT...

!
YES... LIGHT HAS RETURNED TO THE SHIKON JEWEL!
BLUP

HEH HEH HEH... I WONDER HOW THEY ARE OCCU-PIED AT THE MOMENT...
...AND WHAT WILL PASS THROUGH THEIR MINDS WHEN THEY GLIMPSE THE LIGHT.

YOU MEAN... MIROKU? AND SANGO?!

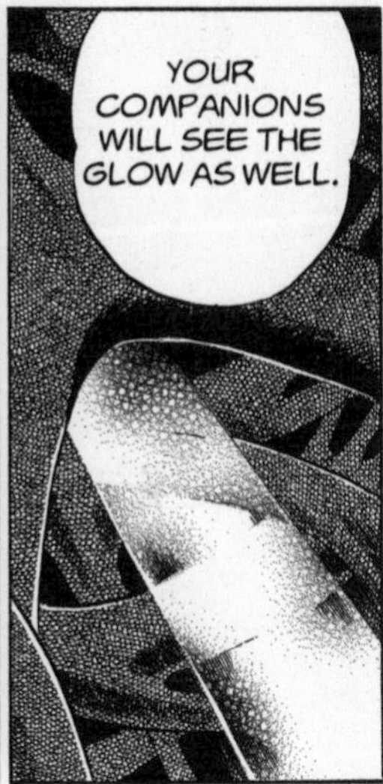
YOUR COMPANIONS WILL SEE THE GLOW AS WELL.

HUH...?!
WHAT DO YOU MEAN?!

ONE THING IS CER-TAIN...
MIROKU'S WIND TUNNEL IS AT ITS LIMIT.
I SUSPECT THE NEXT TIME HE TRIES TO USE IT...
!

HOOOOOOOO

THE TREM-ORS... HAVE STOPPED.

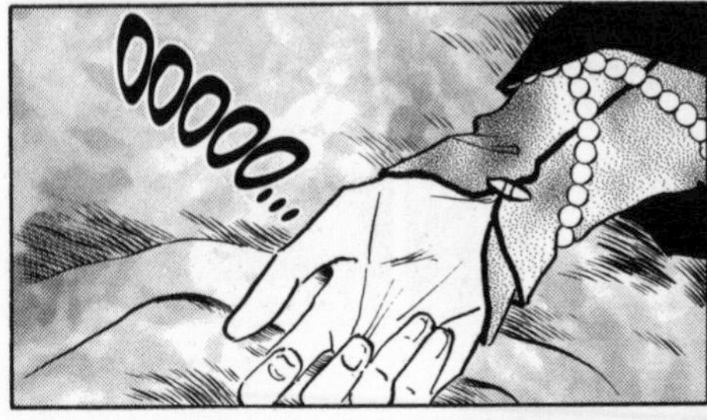
OOOOO...

WHAT NOW...?
I COULD JUST LET LOOSE THE WIND TUNNEL HERE AND NOW...
...TO SEE IF IT DID NARAKU SOME INJURY...

HEH. IT'S IRONIC...
I'M INSIDE NARAKU, AND YET I CANNOT DEAL HIM A MORTAL BLOW!

COULD IT BE...?
...A PURE LIGHT AT THAT!

LIGHT?!

!

IT IS! THE LIGHT OF THE SHIKON JEWEL!
HAVE LADY KAGOME'S POWERS RETURNED?!

AT THE SOURCE OF THAT LIGHT IS THE JEWEL...
HOOO...
...AND NARAKU!

HEH HEH HEH... WHAT A PITY IT WOULD BE...
...IF THE LIGHT HE FOLLOWED FAILED TO LEAD HIM BACK TO ME.

YOU'RE GOING TO TRICK HIM INTO USING THE WIND TUNNEL?!
KKRKRKKRK
YOU WON'T BE IN TIME.
YOUR LIGHT, KAGOME...
...WILL BE THE DEATH OF YOUR COMPAN-IONS.

SCROLL 3
A TRAP OF LIGHT

WOK

DAMN! IT WON'T BUDGE!

WHAT NOW?!
SHOULD WE HEAD FOR THE SHIKON JEWEL TO TAKE NARAKU DOWN FIRST, OR...

INU-YASHA!
WE'VE GOT TO FIND MIROKU!

HEH HEH HEH...
IT SEEMS KAGOME IS ON TOP OF THINGS.
NARA-KU!

OH... ONE MORE THING.
MIROKU HAS LEFT SANGO AND WANDERS ALONE.

I PRESUME HE FEARS SHE MIGHT FALL VICTIM TO HIS WIND TUNNEL.

MIROKU IS... ALONE?

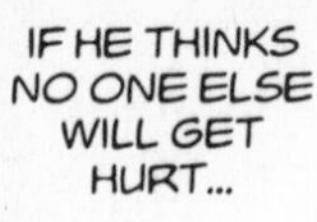
IF HE THINKS NO ONE ELSE WILL GET HURT...

...HE MIGHT DECIDE TO USE THE WIND TUNNEL... ONE LAST TIME!

SPLCH

NARAKU IS AT THE SOURCE OF THAT LIGHT.
SO UNTIL I GET THERE...

HOOOOO
...I BEG YOU, WIND...DO NOT BURST FREE!

HEH HEH HEH... ONE RUSHES TO HIS DEATH, HAVING CHOSEN A LAST RESTING PLACE.
WHILE THE OTHER FEARS THE FIRST'S DEATH MORE THAN ANYTHING IN THE WORLD.
MONK!
MONK!

HOOO...

FMP

MONK...

SANGO... HERE, WE MUST PART WAYS.

BUT... WHY?

ARE YOU PLANNING TO DIE ALONE?

IF YOU DIE, MONK...
...I DIE TOO!

TING...

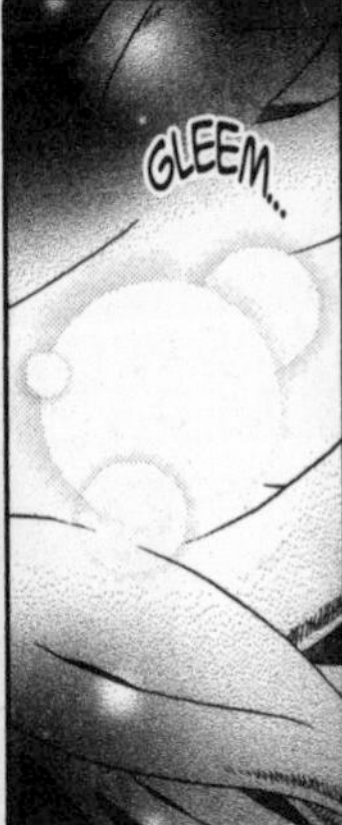
GLEEM...

A LIGHT ...?
COULD IT BE...

...THE LIGHT OF THE JEWEL?!
SHF...

IT MUST BE!
WHICH MEANS THAT AT ITS SOURCE MUST BE... NARAKU!

THE MONK ONCE SAID...
WSH

IF NARAKU DIES, THE CURSE WILL BE UNDONE...
...AND THE WIND TUNNEL WILL DISAPPEAR!

IF I DEFEAT NARAKU...
...I'LL SAVE MIROKU'S LIFE!

B-DOMM

BOOM

KRK
KRK

?!

BLUP

RIN!

WELL, WELL, SANGO... IT SEEMS YOU WIN THE RACE.
YOU ARE THE FIRST TO REACH ME.

GO AHEAD THEN. DESTROY ME.
ALONG WITH THE JEWEL.

LET RIN GO!

WHY? BECAUSE YOU CAN'T THROW HIRAIKOTSU WITH HER IN THE WAY?
NOT EVEN TO KILL THE MIGHTY NARAKU HIMSELF?

OH, DEAR, KIND, GENTLE SANGO...
TOO BAD YOUR KIND-NESS...

WHAT DO YOU MEAN...?!
MUST I SPELL IT OUT? YOU OF ALL PEOPLE SHOULD KNOW.
THE MONK IS CHASING AFTER A FALSE LIGHT. HE IMAGINES HE IS CLOSING IN ON ME.
AT ANY MOMENT, HE IS SURE TO UNLEASH THE WIND TUNNEL...

...WILL BE THE DEATH OF THE MONK.
!

SQUANDERING HIS FINAL ATTACK...AND HIS VERY LIFE...ON A MERE ILLUSION.
SLCH

THE LIGHT GROWS STRONGER...
JUST A LITTLE FARTHER...

SLCH
GLEEM...

B-DMM

HOOOO
NARAKU ...

IT SEEMS YOU WIN THE RACE.
YOU ARE THE FIRST TO REACH ME.

VMMM
THIS WAY!

WE'RE CLOSE!
I SMELL MIROKU!

HE'S MOVING FARTHER AND FARTHER AWAY FROM THE SHIKON JEWEL...

BDM

THIS GIRL RIN...

WHAT IS SHE TO YOU, SANGO?

IS SHE WORTH TRADING FOR THE LIFE OF YOUR BELOVED MONK...?
DAMN YOU...
NGH...

WAFT
SIGH. NARAKU CAN BE SO DEMAND-ING...
ALL THESE ILLUSIONS AT ONCE!

THE ONLY THING THAT'S REAL HERE...
...IS THAT GIRL.

EVEN IF IT SENDS ME TO HELL... I HAVE TO SAVE HIM!

GRP

BDM

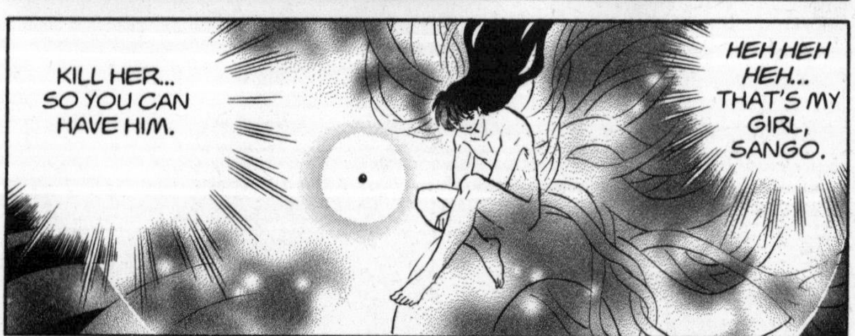

SCROLL 4

LIGHT DEVOURED

VSH

MIROKU! DON'T YOU DARE USE THAT TUNNEL!

BDM
KLATTER...
MIROKU!

EVEN IF THE WIND TUNNEL SPLITS HERE...

FEH!

DIAMOND SPEARS!

TKTKTK

WSH
WHY THE HESITATION, MONK?
DO YOU TREASURE YOUR LIFE, AFTER ALL?

CURSE YOU!
DMM

WHAT?!
SWOO

HSH

CAN'T MIROKU SEE US?!
HE DIDN'T REACT TO THE DIAMOND SPEARS EITHER.

THE ONLY THING HE'S AWARE OF IS THE FAKE NARAKU!
NARAKU'S TRYING TO GET US SUCKED INTO THE WIND TUNNEL WITH HIS ILLUSION!

HOOO

THIS IS IT, NARAKU!

FORGIVE ME, SANGO...
I WISH WE COULD HAVE MADE A LIFE TOGETHER!

WIND TUNNEL...
KLATTA

MIROKU!!

I WON'T
LET YOU!!
WP

WAM

NNG...
...
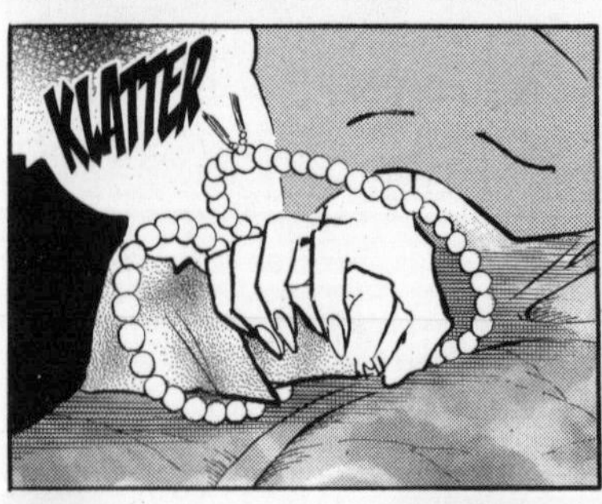
KLATTER

KAGOME! THE ROSARY!
YES!

THAT WAS TOO CLOSE...
IF YOU'D UNLEASHED THAT THING A SECOND SOONER...

HEH HEH HEH... FALTERED AT THE LAST MINUTE, EH?
DEFEATED BY YOUR ATTACHMENT TO THIS WORLD, MONK?
RRGH!

SHUT UP!
I CAN STILL DRAG YOU DOWN WITH ME TO—

SNAP OUT OF IT, MIROKU!
DON'T YOU RECOGNIZE ME?!

THIS ILLUSION...
I HAVE TO BREAK IT...!

TWNG

HEH
HEH
HEH...
SSH
I

IT'S
STILL
THERE
?!

I'M NOT
LEAV-
ING...

...UNTIL
THE
MONK IS
DEAD.
AND I SEE
WHAT
SANGO IS
WILLING TO
DO...
...TO "SAVE"
HIM.
SANGO?!

BOMM

LIGHT ...?!
SLCH SLCH

GLOW
!

BDMM
!

SISTER!

RIN?!

IF THIS IS THE ONLY WAY...TO SAVE THE MONK'S LIFE...

SHE'S GOING TO THROW HIRAI-KOTSU?!
SANGO!
SISTER!
BYA-KUYA!
HELLO, KOHAKU.

JUST BE STILL AND WATCH.
SANGO CAN'T HEAR YOU ANYWAY.

WHAT DO YOU MEAN...?!
HUMAN HEARTS ARE SO WEAK.
ESPECIALLY YOUR BIG SISTER'S— ESPECIALLY NOW.
SHE IS OBLIVIOUS TO ALL. HER ONLY THOUGHT IS HOW TO RESCUE HER MONK.

THIS IS THE ONLY CHANCE I HAVE TO STOP HIM...
...FROM UNLEASHING THE WIND TUNNEL...

...AND GETTING SWAL-LOWED UP LIKE HIS FATHER!
AH, SANGO. YOUR FEAR AND FRAILTY...
...RESON-ATE NICELY WITH THE DARKNESS OF THE JEWEL.

EVEN IF IT MEANS SACRIFICING RIN...
WSH

!

THE SHIKON JEWEL'S DARKNESS...

...IS PUSHING AGAINST MY CLEANSING LIGHT?!

!
HEH HEH HEH... IT SEEMS SANGO HAS FALLEN.

THE LIGHT IS BEING DE-VOURED!

I HAVE TO STOP IT...
...BEFORE NARAKU REGAINS HIS POWER!

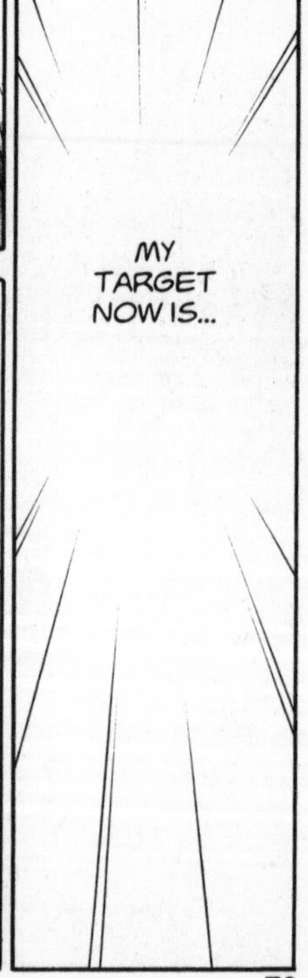
MY TARGET NOW IS...

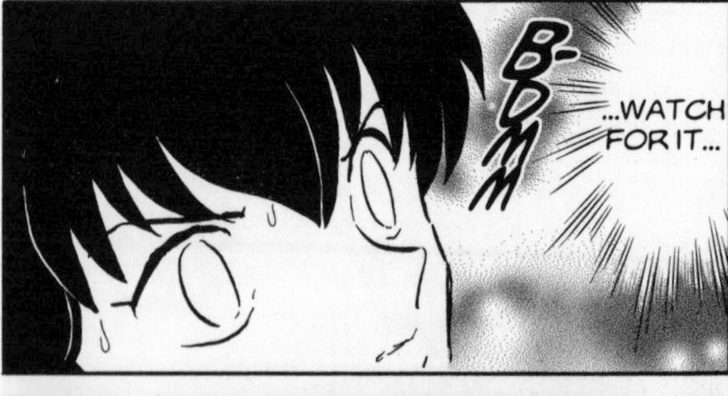
B-DOMM
...WATCH FOR IT...

HOOOO...
KAGO-ME...?!

GLEEM...

BDMM
I SEE IT!
KRIIIK...

HRR

FORGIVE ME, RIN!

SANGO!

SCROLL 5
THE VANISHING ARROW

VSH

BDM
HEH HEH HEH...

WHEN SANGO'S WEAPON RIPS THROUGH LITTLE RIN...

...THE JEWEL WILL BE FULLY STEEPED IN DARKNESS ONCE MORE.
SWOOO...

NARAKU!

TING

KAGOME!
WHAT DID
YOU JUST
SHOOT AT?!

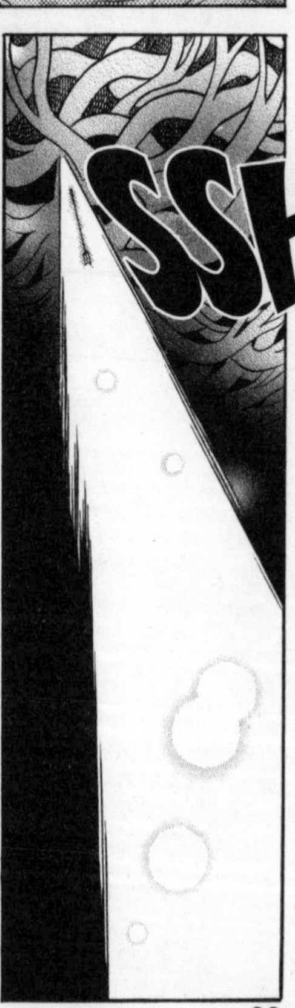
SSH

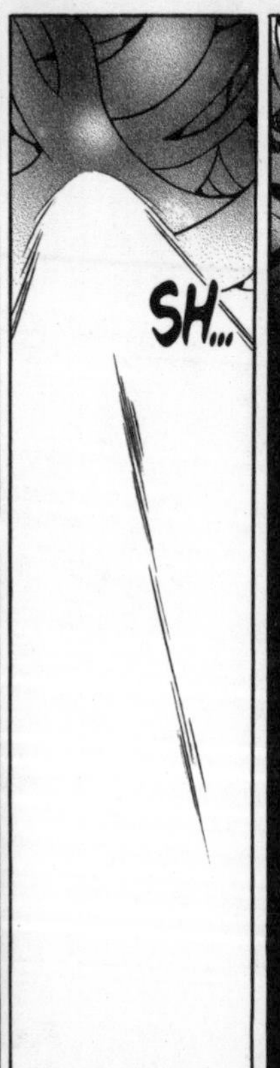
SH...

YOUR
ARROW...
VANISHED?!

JUST LIKE
BEFORE!

VOOO

...REACH NARAKU!

DO-OM

KRII KRIII

RRRIP

SHLUP
!

RIN!
HOOM

WMP

KOHAKU...

SANGO!
RIN IS SAFE!

B-DOMM

BIG SIS...

YOU THREW HIRAIKOTSU... KNOWING THAT RIN WOULD DIE...DIDN'T YOU?

YOU MERELY STRUCK THE ILLUSION OF NARAKU I SHOWED YOU.

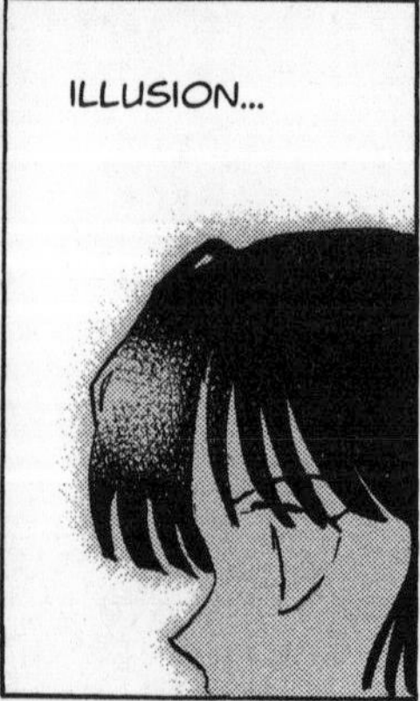
ILLUSION...

YOU DECIDED THAT THIS INNOCENT GIRL SHOULD BE SACRIFICED...

...SO THAT YOU COULD HAVE YOUR BOYFRIEND.
I...

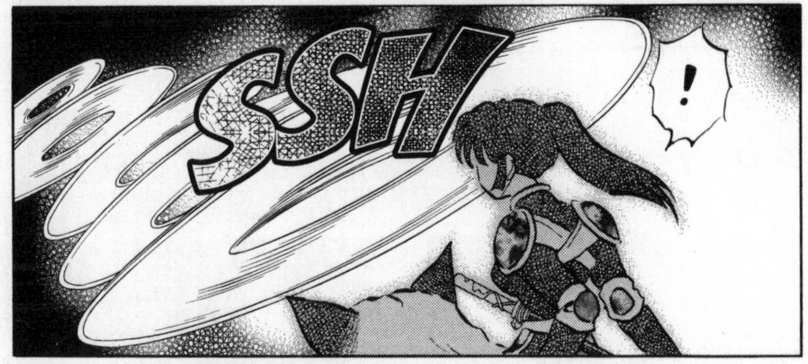
!
SSH

WOOP!
ZWIF

TK TK TK TK TK TK

?!

HWAAA
LORD SESSHO-MARU!

SESSHO-
MARU...

IF YOU MEAN TO STRIKE ME, YOU'LL HAVE TO AIM BETTER THAN THAT.
BDM

FROM THE LOOK ON YOUR FACE, I TAKE IT YOU OVER-HEARD US.
WELL, I'LL LET YOU TWO SETTLE THIS BETWEEN YOUR-SELVES.
SPLCH SPLCH
TA-TA!

NOW *THAT* WAS A SURPRISE.
MY PROGENITOR ACTUALLY TOOK AN ARROW.
SLCH

BUT SINCE HIS OFF-SHOOT—ME—IS STILL HERE...

...THAT MEANS BOTH NARAKU AND THE JEWEL ARE ALIVE AND WELL.

BDMMM
SESSHO-MARU...

BUT I WAS ABOUT TO KILL HER!

SHE WAS TRICKED BY ILLUSIONS!
B-DOMM

THAT DOESN'T CHANGE THE FACT THAT I CHOSE TO SACRIFICE RIN.
I CHOSE KILLING NARAKU OVER EVERYTHING.

BUT, SIS-TER...
I DON'T INTEND TO MAKE EXCUSES OR BEG FOR MY LIFE.

ALL I ASK...

...IS THAT YOU WAIT UNTIL WE DEFEAT NARAKU AND...
BDMM
...UNDO THE CURSE OF THE WIND TUNNEL.
SANGO...

VMMM

B-DMMM

INU-YASHA ...
...PUT ME DOWN!
FORGET IT!

IF I LEAVE YOU ALONE, WHO KNOWS WHEN THE NEXT ILLUSION WILL SUCKER YOU INTO USING THE WIND TUNNEL!

WE'RE ALL GETTING THROUGH THIS...*ALIVE!*

VMMM

SCROLL 6
THE CENTER

1

DOOM
PL-PLUP
PLUP
PLUP
PLUPP
PLUPP
SWOO

IT'S GETTING BRIGHTER...

THE AIR SMELLS... DIFFERENT.
TOWARD THAT LIGHT...
...THAT'S WHERE THE REAL NARAKU IS!

VM

WE'VE GOT TO FOLLOW HIM, SIS!
...YES.

I GATHER THIS MEANS...
...HE'S WILLING TO WAIT UNTIL WE DEFEAT NARAKU... BEFORE HE...

I WANT TO SEE HIM—ONE LAST TIME!

WSH

PL-PLUP PL-PLUP

!!

SPLCH

SWOO...
THERE'S LIGHT IN THE JEWEL AGAIN!

I'M SENDING YOU AND YOUR JEWEL STRAIGHT TO THE UNDERWORLD!

B-DMM

MEIDO
ZANGE-
TSUHA...
VSH
WOOM
!

VVVP
AAAAH!
HEH HEH... MISSED ME.
HOOO

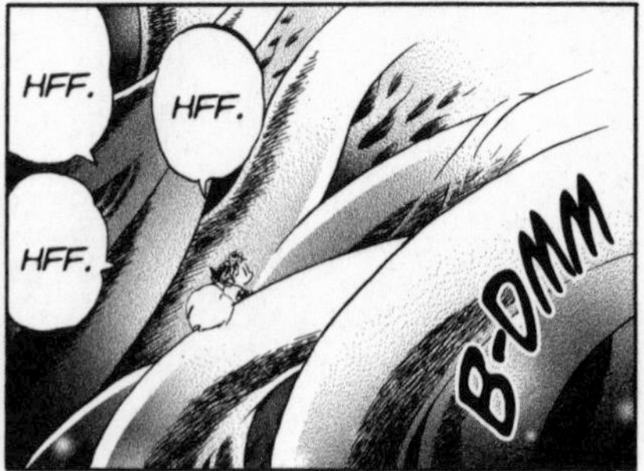
HFF.
HFF.
HFF.
B-DMM

THERE'S SOME-THING... OVER THERE...
LIGHT!

HOOO...
HUH?!

OOM
AGH!!

TH-THAT'S INU-YASHA'S...
...MEIDO ZANGE-TSUHA!
HOOOOO
TP TP TP TP

!
HOOOOO
SLCH

AND THAT'S ...
...BYAKUYA OF THE DREAMS...
PEEK
SIGH...
SO THE TIME HAS FINALLY COME FOR ME TO DRAW THIS.
SHW

HUH?!
THERE'S NO BLADE?!

VVVMMMN

B-DMVM

WHOA!
THERE IS NOW...

HELLO.

YOU CAN'T HIDE FROM ME, SILLY.

W-WHAT THE...?
WHAT DID YOU JUST DO?!

YOU WERE WATCH-ING, WEREN'T YOU?
I STOLE THE MEIDO ZANGETSUHA'S POWER.
AS NARAKU COM-MANDED.

STOLE... ITS POWER?!
SURE YOU DID!
INUYASHA AND SESSHOMARU HAD TO WORK LIKE HELL TO MASTER THAT MOVE!
YOU CAN'T JUST TAKE IT LIKE THAT!

THAT'S WHY...
...THIS BLADE MAY BE USED ONLY ONCE.

I HAVE NO IDEA HOW NARAKU PLANS TO WIELD IT...
...BUT THIS SIGNIFIES THE END IS NEAR.

IF YOU WERE THINKING OF SCAMPER-ING AWAY...
NOW'S YOUR CHANCE.
SSSLRB
HUH?

HE'S... IGNORING ME?!

H-HE'S ...
...NOT EVEN GONNA TRY TO CAPTURE ME OR ANYTHING?

BOOF
BYE-BYE!

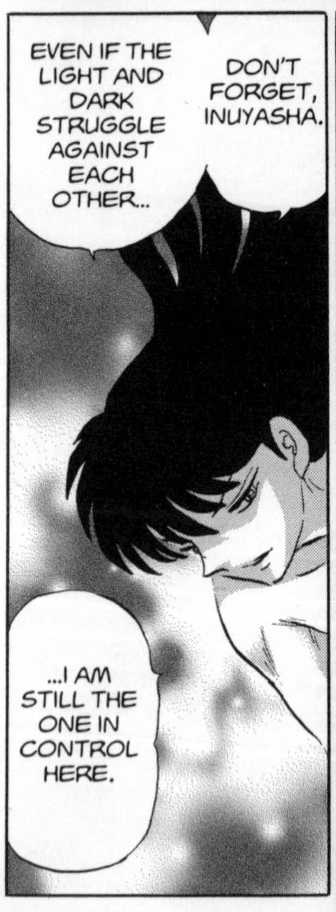
DON'T FORGET, INUYASHA.
EVEN IF THE LIGHT AND DARK STRUGGLE AGAINST EACH OTHER...
...I AM STILL THE ONE IN CONTROL HERE.

HEH HEH HEH ...
SLB SLB
BDDM

QUIT BLUFFING!
BDM

!
BLUP

MIASMA!
SSSS...

DAMN!
VSH

DZT
INU-YASHA!
ZZZ

BDMM
THIS MIASMA IS DIFFERENT...
THIS ONE CAN KILL YOU ALL.

ESPECIALLY THE WEAKLING HUMANS LIKE...
...KAGOME AND THE MONK.
ZZSS
RRH!

YOU DON'T EVEN CARE ABOUT YOUR APPEARANCE ANYMORE?
FEELING THE PRESSURE, ARE YOU, NARAKU?

NARAKU IS TRYING TO PREVENT ME FROM SHOOTING!
HE'S AFRAID OF MY ARROWS.

BDMM

YOU'RE SAFE NOW.
LORD SESSHO-MARU!

ARE YOU AWAKE, RIN?
KOHA-KU...

NNH...

BLUP
!

BIG SIS!

SSH

WHAT...? MIASMA ?!
ZZSS

RIN...
I'M SO SORRY ...

WHAT ...?

...

SIS-TER!
YOU'RE NOT WEARING YOUR MASK!
VM
I'LL GO ON AHEAD!

WHY DOES SHE RISK HER LIFE...?

SCROLL 7

DESPAIR

WSH

HURTS... TO BREATHE ...
SWOO...
FEELS LIKE THE MIASMA IS GETTING STRONGER...

LORD SESSHO-MARU! PLEASE GO AFTER LADY SANGO!

THE MIASMA WILL KILL HER!

SHK
SHK
!

WHA ...?!

HMPH.
IT APPEARS HE DOESN'T WANT US TO CATCH UP TO HER.

VSH
B-DMM

PLEASE WAIT FOR ME, MONK!

ooo
BDMM
!

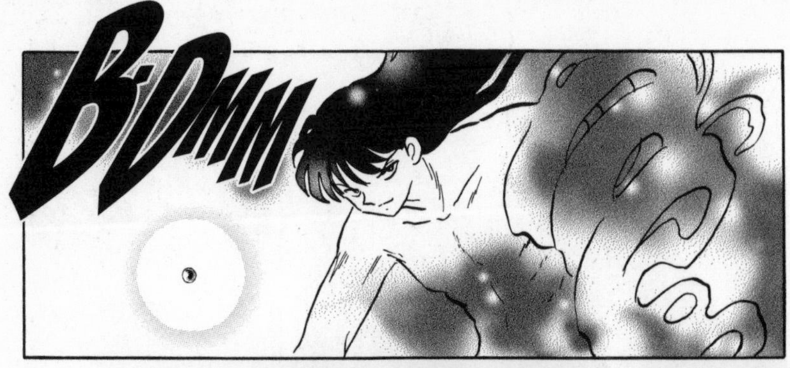
B-DMM

NARAKU!

RELIEVED, SANGO...?
THE MONK IS STILL ALIVE.

SANGO!
B-DMM
SANGO!

B'DMMM
SANGO
...

HE'S ALIVE!

I MADE IT IN TIME...

SANGO, PUT ON YOUR MASK!
NARAKU'S TRYING TO KILL US WITH HIS MIASMA!!

MIASMA OR EVIL AURA...
...I'LL DESTROY IT ALL!
VSH

HIRAI-KOTSU!

WRR

VRR RRR
HOO

FUNNELS OF MIASMA?!

TK TK TK TK

HAVE YOU FORGOT-TEN, NARAKU?!
MY HIRAIKOTSU TEARS APART EVIL AURAS!

SNAP SNAP

GRP

SSH...

WSH
TWNG

NO!
BOOOM
SAN-
GO!

SANGO IS ALREADY WELL DRENCHED IN MY MIASMA.

IT'S TOO LATE TO CLEANSE IT NOW.

MIROKU!
SANGO!

KAGO-
ME!
WMP

YEEE!
CHAK
CHAK

SSH
RGH!

SHHM
RRRIP

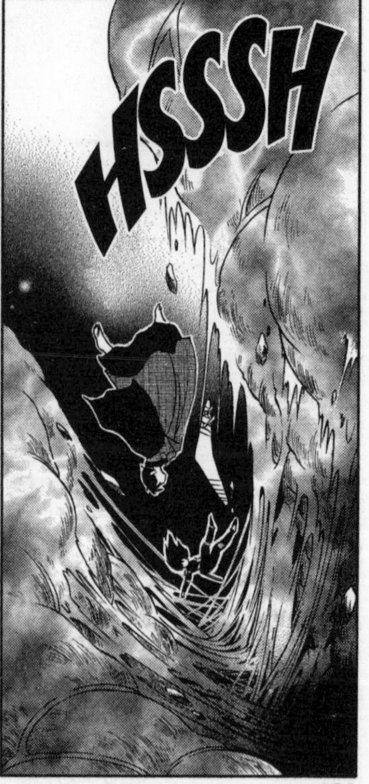
HSSSH

HEH HEH HEH... YOU REALLY OUGHT TO LET THEM SPEND THEIR LAST MOMENTS TOGETHER IN PRIVATE...
B-BOM

HOO8
NO...

SAN-GO!

WFF

SAN-GO...

WHY ...?

HOOOOO...

THE SOUND...
OF THE WIND
TUNNEL...

SO I'VE
FAILED...

MONK
...

SANGO...
I'M SO
SORRY...
...TO
ABAN-
DON
YOU...

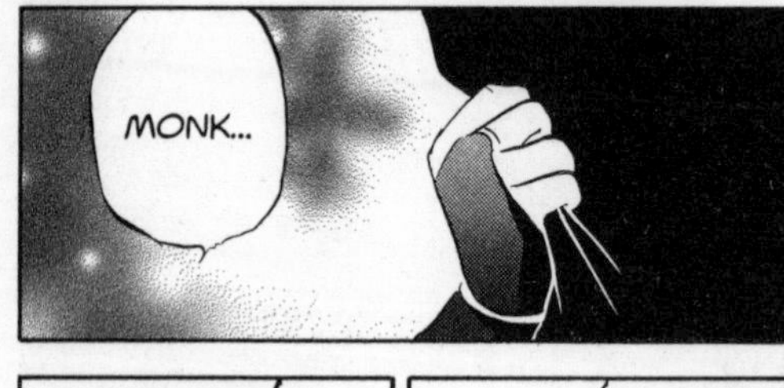
MONK...

TAKE
ME...
WITH
YOU...

SANGO
...

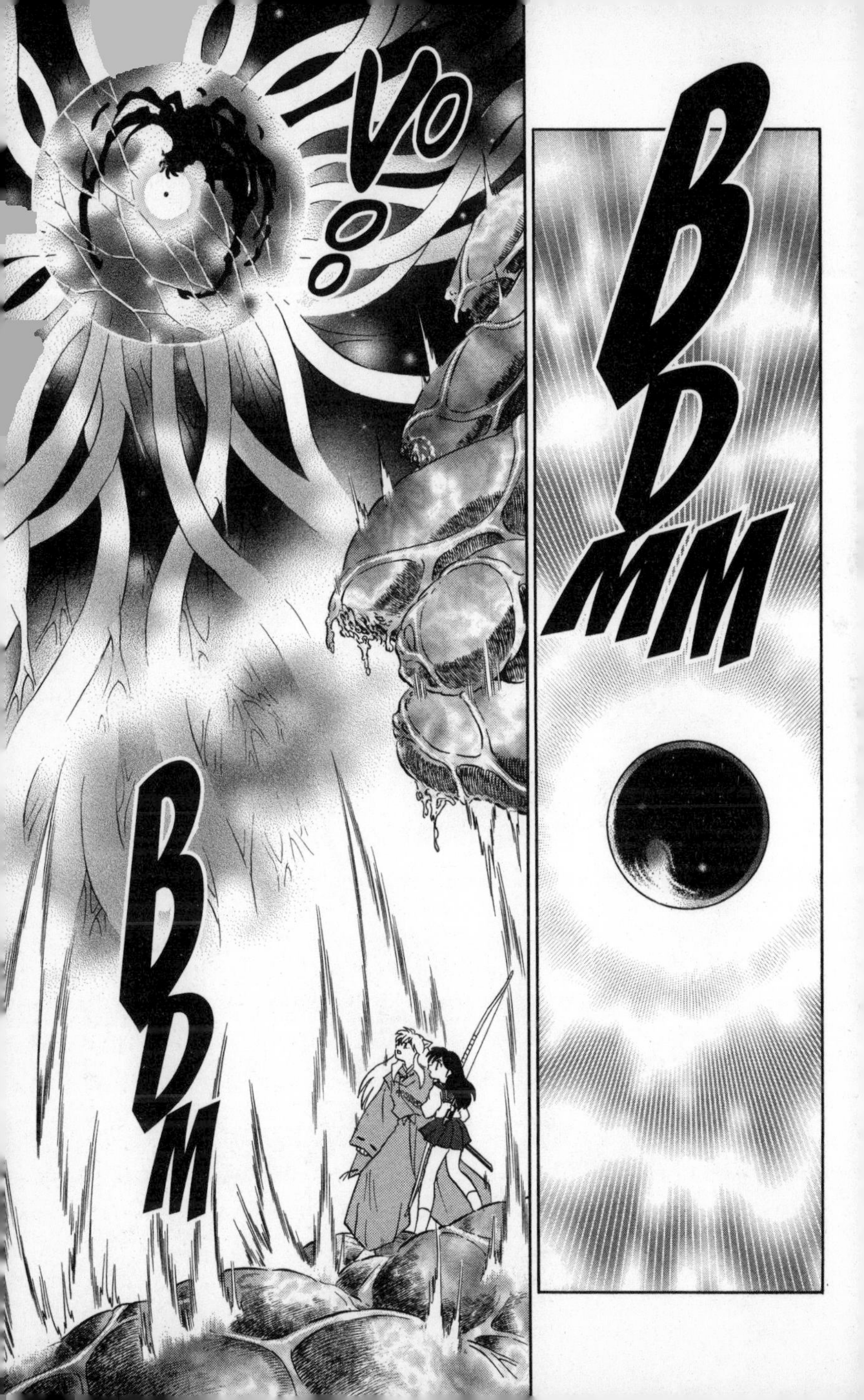

BDMM
VOOO
BDM

HEH HEH HEH.
THEIR SORROW FEEDS THE DARKNESS...
B-DMMM
SLCH SLCH
SLCH SLCH

NARAKU!
HOW IRONIC... THE MORE THEY LOVE EACH OTHER...
...THE DEEPER THEIR DESPAIR ...
YOU...
B-DOM
GNG...

...YOU WILL DEFEAT NARAKU!

BDM

SCROLL 8
NARAKU'S DESIRE

DYING TOGETHER FOR LOVE... HOW DELICIOUS THAT...

...WHEN THEY BREATHE THEIR LAST...

...THEY WILL BE ***DEVOURED*** BY THE DARKNESS OF THE SHIKON JEWEL.

BDMM

I WON'T LET THAT HAPPEN!
NARAKU, I WILL TAKE YOU DOWN, DESTROY YOU...
...AND END THE CURSE OF THE WIND TUNNEL!
MEIDO ZANGE-TSUHA!
WSH
BDM

DOOOM

SWSH

DOOM

!
HE'S NOT GETTING PULLED INTO THE MEIDO?!

THIS IS THE POWER OF THE SHIKON JEWEL.
KRIII

THE JEWEL THAT WAS MEANT TO BURN WITH KIKYO'S REMAINS...
...AND VANISH FOR-EVER FROM THIS WORLD.

BUT IT'S A CLEVER JEWEL ...

IT USED KIKYO'S REGRET TOWARD ***YOU***, INUYASHA...

...TO BE REBORN INSIDE KAGOME'S BODY AND RETURN TO THIS WORLD.

SO EVEN IF WE KILL...
NARAKU... ANSWER ME!

WHAT DO YOU REALLY WANT?

KAGOME...?

THE WHOLE TIME YOU'VE BEEN BATTLING US...

...IT'S SEEMED LIKE YOU HAVE ONLY ONE GOAL IN MIND.

YOU TORE INUYASHA AND KIKYO APART...

...FORCED SANGO AND KOHAKU TO FIGHT EACH OTHER...

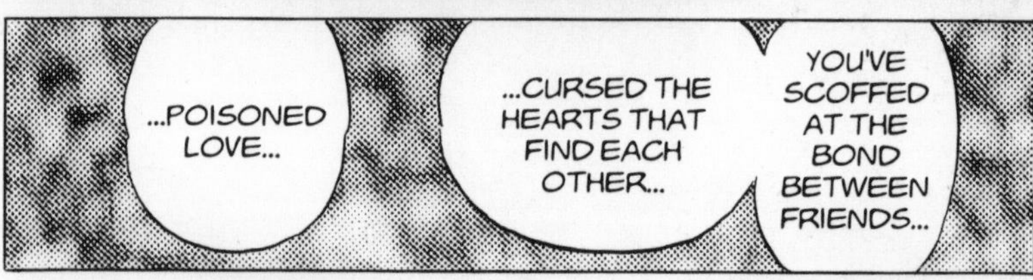

YOU'D HAVE TO KNOW HOW PRECIOUS THOSE BONDS ARE...

...TO KNOW THE PAIN OF LOSING THEM.

THE SHIKON JEWEL...
...DIDN'T GRANT YOU YOUR TRUEST DESIRE, DID IT?
BMMM

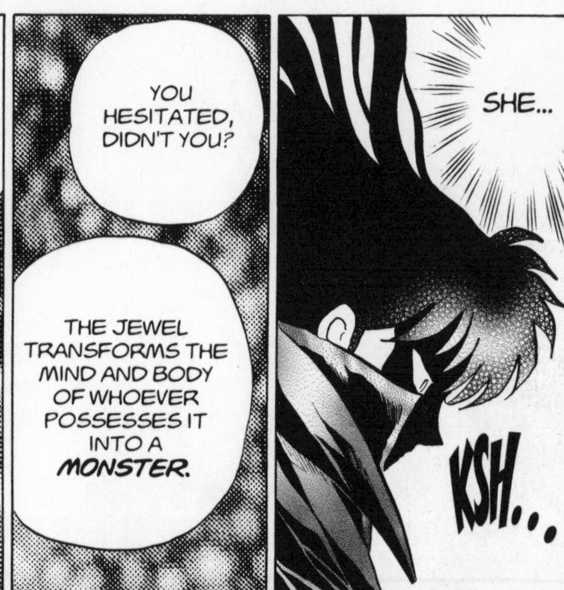

SO WHAT...?

KAGOME, YOU...

YOU SAW THROUGH ME...

DON'T TELL ME YOU THINK TO...
PAH
...WEAKEN ME WITH WORDS?!

MIASMA SPEARS!
VM
KAGOME, STAND BACK!!

MEIDO ZANGE-TSUHA!

WSH

BOOM

SHM

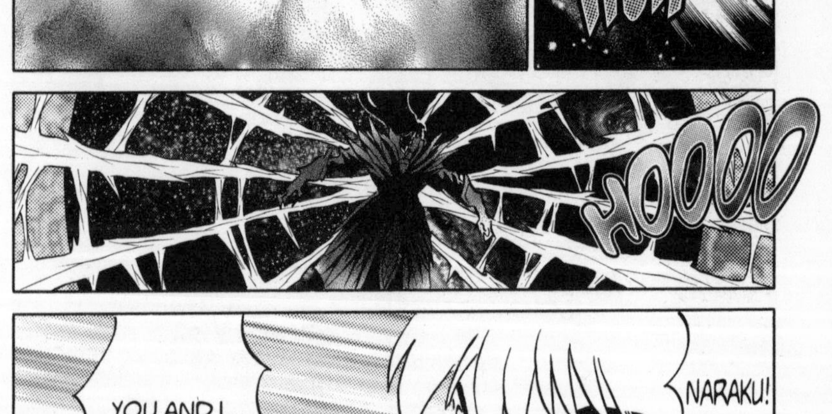

NARAKU!

YOU AND I...

...WERE SPAWNED DIFFERENTLY, BUT WE'RE BOTH HALF DEMON!

WE POSSESS BOTH A HUMAN AND A DEMON HEART!

THAT'S WHY I AM DESTINED TO KILL YOU!!

I WON'T LET YOU...
...HURT MY FRIENDS ANYMORE!
HWSH
ZAH

ZAH

SCROLL 9
A CUTTING MEIDO

HOOO

THE MEIDO BECAME...A BLADE...

B-DMM

THE SHIKON JEWEL!

IF I PIERCE IT, NARAKU WILL BE DESTROYED!!
KRIII

AH!

SHK SHK
OOM
OH!!

KAGO-ME!!
HHF

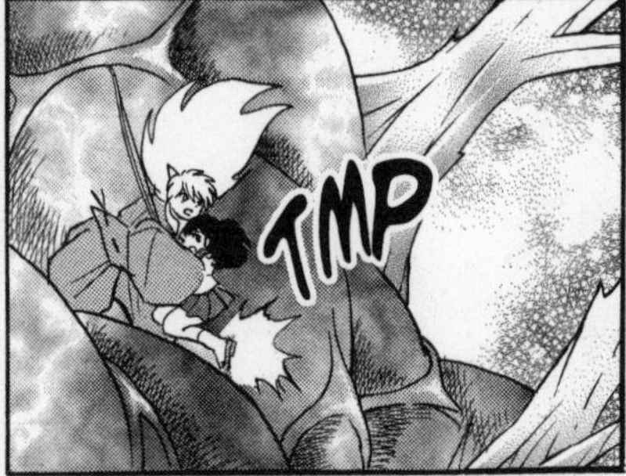
TMP

SHOO...
SPLCH SPLCH

IT'S NO USE...
SPLCH
I'LL JUST KEEP REGENERAT-ING OVER AND OVER AGAIN.

OH YEAH ?!
THEN I'LL JUST KEEP CUTTING YOU DOWN!

HOOOOO
SO. THE MEIDO ZANGE-TSUHA...
...HAS TRANS-FORMED.

TOTO-SAI...
DOES THIS MEAN INUYASHA HAS FINALLY MADE THAT MOVE HIS OWN?
YES.

SESSHOMARU HONED THE MEIDO ZANGETSUHA WITH TENSEIGA, "THE BLADE THAT DOES NOT CUT."
OPENING A GIGANTIC MEIDO TO KILL HIS ENEMIES...THAT'S SESSHOMARU'S STYLE.

SO IN ORDER FOR INUYASHA TO MASTER IT...
...THE SWORD, THE SWORDS-MAN, AND THE MOVE HAD TO **BECOME ONE.**

AND TETSU-SAIGA...
...IS A CUTTING BLADE.
B-DMMM

BUT I'LL SEVER IT ALL FOR YOU. INCLUDING...

...YOUR BOND WITH THE SHIKON JEWEL!

MEIDO ZANGE-TSUHA!!

SHIM

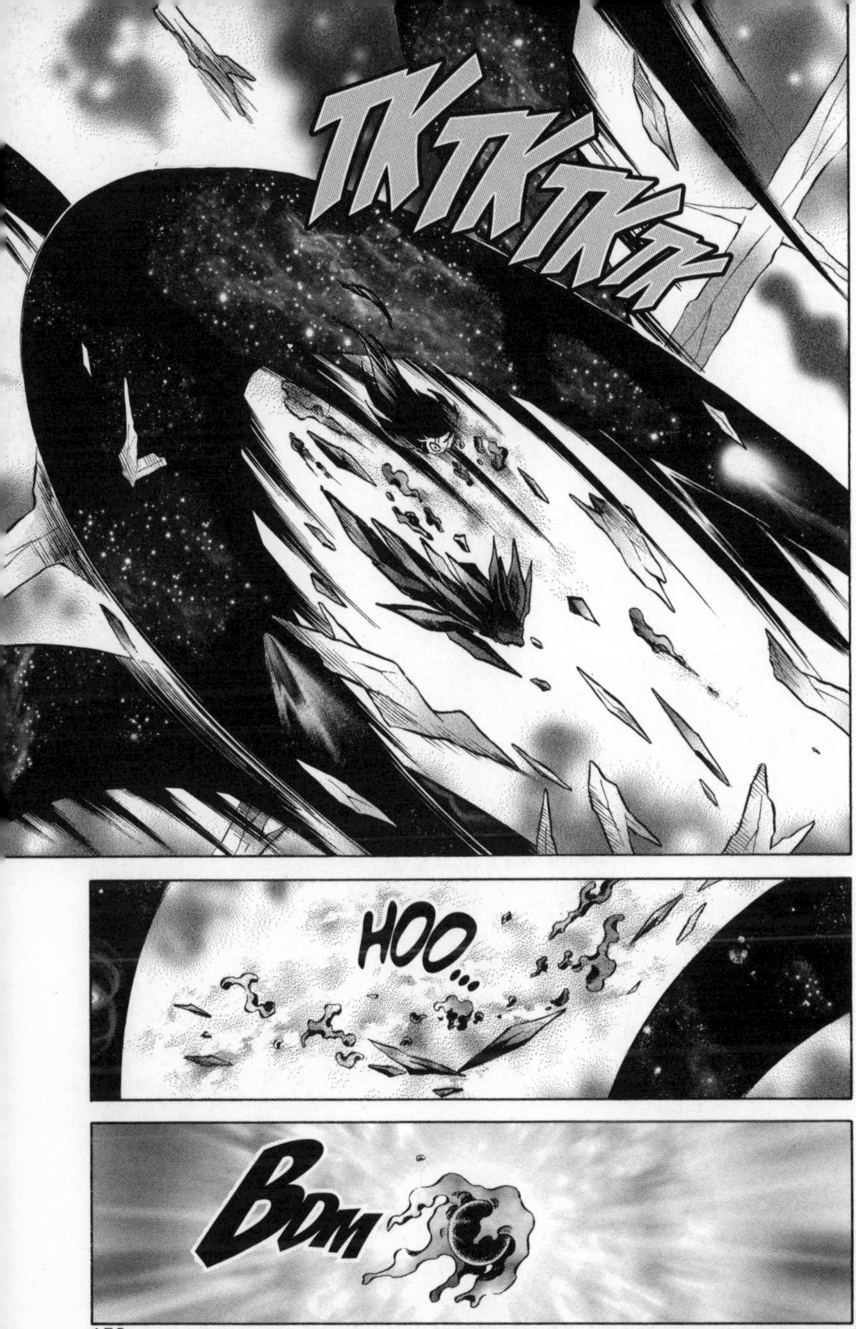

TKTKTKTK

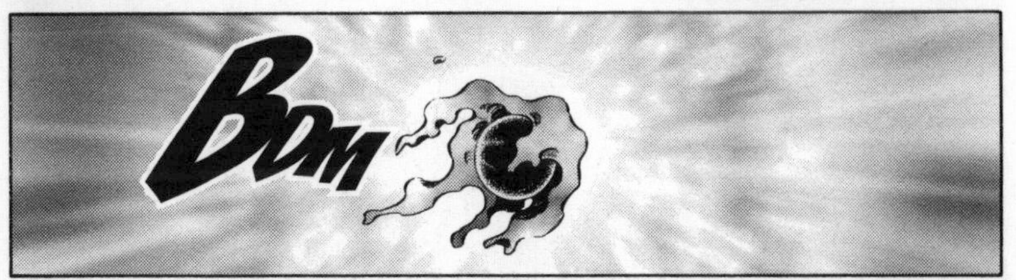

OHH!
ZZSSS
BLP
BLP

MONK...

TAKE ME WITH YOU...

W-W-WHAT?!
B'DOM
BL-BLUP
OWWWWW!
MIASMA!
DZTZZSS
I KNEW I SHOULDN'T HAVE COME!
ALL ALONE, ABANDONED BY THE OTHERS, AND...
B'BOM
LORD SESSHOMARU!

HWSH
THE MIASMA IS GETTING STRONGER!

SOMETHING IS HAPPENING...
IT MUST BE... INUYASHA.
ARE YOU FINALLY CORNERED, NARAKU...?
IN THAT CASE...
...I SHALL DELIVER YOUR COUP DE GRACE!
BAKUSAIGA!
HWA

A PATH HAS OPENED UP!
W-WOW...

VM

EVEN AFTER SESSHOMARU'S BLADE STOPS CUTTING, IT CONTINUES TO SOW DESTRUCTION...

...IN THE BODIES OF WHOSOEVER HAS ABSORBED ITS POWER.

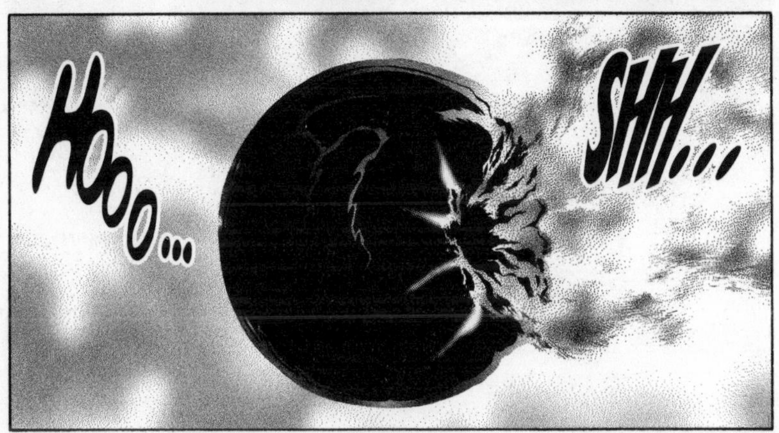

HUH?
WHAT NOW?

AGH!

DM
OH!

FWA
LORD SESSHO-MARU!!

WOK

LORD JAKEN...! YOU'RE HERE?
WHERE HAVE YOU BEEN HIDING?
SHUT UP!

DM DM DM DM DM

THAT SOUND...

NARA-KU!
YOU WON'T BE ABLE...
...TO REGEN-ERATE ANYMORE!
HEH...

I THOUGHT I TOLD YOU, INUYASHA ...
...EVEN IF I PERISH... THE JEWEL SHALL NOT DISAPPEAR...

SKWK SKWK
B-DMM

SCROLL 10

BYAKUYA'S BLADE

HOOO

BLUP BLUP

SOMETHING... HAS BEGUN.

DDDDD

SPRT
POP
!

THE MIASMA ...
KWCH
KWCH
...IS REACHING ITS SATURATION POINT!

SANGO ...

ZZZ...
DDDDDD

IF I USE THE WIND TUNNEL...
...I COULD SUCK AWAY ALL THIS MIASMA...

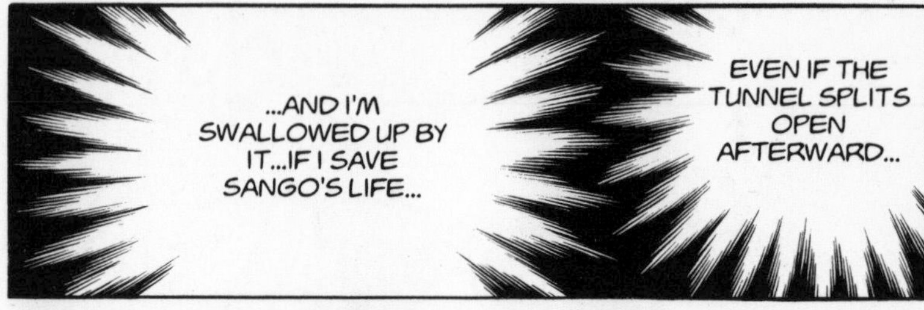
EVEN IF THE TUNNEL SPLITS OPEN AFTERWARD...
...AND I'M SWALLOWED UP BY IT...IF I SAVE SANGO'S LIFE...

!
THE TUNNEL... IT'S...

RRM
!
DM DM

HUF...
HUF...
HUF...
B-DM
B-DM

THE DESTRUCTION IS GROWING CLOSER!
I'VE GOTTA BE QUICK OR I'LL GET CAUGHT UP IN IT!!

H-HE'S BREAKING APART!
DZZD

SHOO...
!

WUP

K-KIRARA?!

TNK

REEL

ARGH!!

SWOO
GAH!

AMAZ-
ING...
THE DEVAS-
TATION
KEEPS
SPREAD-
ING.
AND HE ONLY
STRUCK
ONCE...
THAT'S MY LORD
SESSHOMARU'S
BLADE FOR
YOU! IN A CLASS
OF ITS OWN!

KRAK KRAK

HEH...
NARAKU...
STILL
RESIST-
ING,
EH...?
BAKU-
SAIGA!
HWA

GIVE IT UP, NARAKU ...
IT'S OVER.

HEH...
IT DOES APPEAR THAT WAY...

YEAH ?!
YOU WANT TO TRY ME?!

YOU MEAN ...
...YOUR **SOUL**, DON'T YOU?

HOOO
BUT, INU-YASHA...
...YOU OUGHT TO KNOW THERE ARE SOME THINGS THAT NEITHER...
...YOUR TETSUSAIGA NOR SESSHO-MARU'S BAKUSAIGA CAN SEVER.

THAT'S WHAT I'M HERE FOR!
TO CLEANSE YOUR SOUL, NARAKU!

THAT'S RIGHT, KAGOME ...
THE FINAL STRUGGLE WILL BE...A BATTLE OF SOULS!

WSH...
!

HOOO

WHAT...? THAT BLADE...

IT CONTAINS THE MEIDO ZANGE-TSUHA?!

BOOM

ZASH

KSHINK

HEH...
WUP...
AS HIS INCARNATION, I WILL PERISH ANYWAY WHEN NARAKU DIES.
I HAVE NO RE-GRETS.

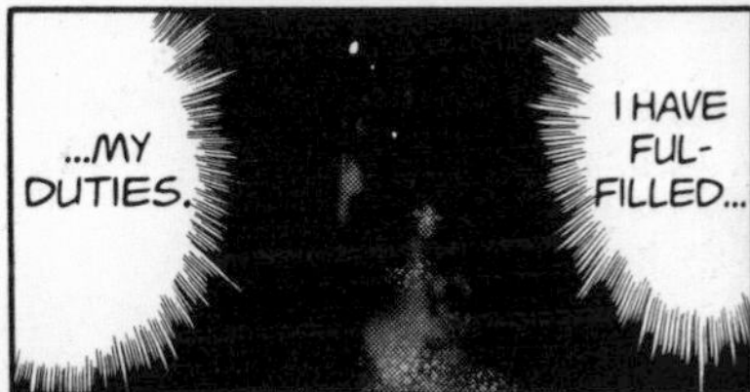
I HAVE FUL-FILLED...
...MY DUTIES.

HOOOO

KAGO-
ME!
BOMM

ARE YOU ALL RIGHT?!
Y-YEAH...

WHAT DID HE DO?
THAT BASTARD...

DID I JUST...
...GET CUT...?

HSH

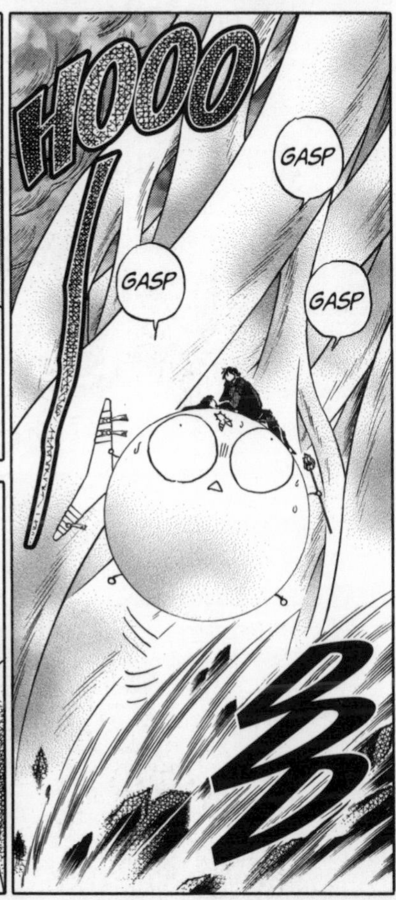
HOOO
GASP
GASP
GASP

THANK YOU, SHIPPO. YOU SAVED US.
Y-YEAH. I KNOW...

YOU TWO SURE ARE BEAT UP THOUGH.
YOU GONNA MAKE IT?

YES...
IT WILL BE OVER SOON...

UNH...

SANGO! ARE YOU AWAKE...?
M... MONK...

DON'T MOVE TOO MUCH!
HOLD STILL OR THE MIASMA'S POISON WILL CIRCULATE...

I'M...ALL RIGHT...
BUT... WHAT ABOUT YOU...?

SANGO...
I CAN STILL FIGHT!

EH...?

I CAN'T HEAR THE WIND TUNNEL ANY-MORE...

MONK! DOES THAT MEAN...
...THE POWER OF NARAKU'S CURSE HAS WEAKENED?!

INUYASHA AND THE OTHERS...
...MUST HAVE DEALT NARAKU A DECISIVE BLOW!

YES!

TO SEVER OUR BONDS WITH NARAKU...

VSH

TO BE CONTINUED...

INUYASHA
VOL. 55
Shonen Sunday Edition

Story and Art by
RUMIKO TAKAHASHI

English Adaptation by Gerard Jones
Translation/Mari Morimoto
Touch-up Art & Lettering/Bill Schuch
Cover & Interior Graphic Design/Yuki Ameda
Editor/Annette Roman

Printed in the U.S.A.

Published by VIZ Media, LLC
P.O. Box 77010
San Francisco, CA 94107

10 9 8 7 6 5 4 3 2 1
First printing, December 2010

PARENTAL ADVISORY
INUYASHA is rated T+ for Older Teen and is recommended for ages 16 and up. This volume contains violence.
ratings.viz.com

www.viz.com WWW.SHONENSUNDAY.COM

TV SERIES & MOVIES ON DVD!

See more of the action in *Inuyasha* full-length movies

www.viz.com
inuyasha.viz.com

INUYASHA

The popular anime series now on DVD—each season available in a collectible box set

INUYASHA SEASON 1

INUYASHA SECOND SEASON BOX SET

INUYASHA THIRD SEASON BOX SET